THE SICKNESS:
Actor-Based Reality

Kat Clarion

BookLeaf Publishing

India | USA | UK

Presentation by *BookLeaf Publishing*

Web: www.bookleafpub.com

E-mail: info@bookleafpub.com

ISBN: 978-93-5744-973-1

First edition 2022

DEDICATION

Dedicated to those whose light shines brightly enough to illuminate dark places.

ACKNOWLEDGEMENT

In acknowledgement of the many minds which have been lost to the Sickness - and in solidarity with those who can see.

"With thanks to Geomatrix, my brother Rob, and the entire Freedom Family."

PREFACE

It's not our fault but it IS our responsibility.

Disbelieving

A butterfly floats in, beautiful.
A butterfly rests on the back of your hand,
while you look away - disbelieving.

Eye of the Beast

The Sickness pervades inside a closed system.
Preferring to reject the solutions that we're given.
Art imitates life - the Truth is stranger than fiction.
Declining autonomy in exchange for wishful thinking.

Warned a thousand ways - but still we didn't listen.
Fixating on spoils of so many stolen generations.
Imitating shapeshifters. Of course, we lost our center.
Hard to drop anchor with an identity that's shattered.

Human minds like firewalls - dealing false security.
Easily distracted by avoiding our obscurity.
The Sickness is a network; many, pluralistic.
Endlessly tormenting and relentlessly sadistic.

Deceiving, inverting and twisting their knots around morals and meaning til the meaning is lost.

Signature pattern: recognize ALL FORMS of
deception.
Making values our armour and morals our
weapons.
Because the Sickness destroys our hope in
redemption
from the battering ram that the Sickness
invented.

They're viruses and we're full of bugs.
Can't sit still unless we're screened out. Or
drugged.
Drama, disguise, illusion - change the station.
It's time to train our senses to detect
manipulation.

Looking for the programs - see the patterns still
repeating.
Raising up our voices and our hands while some
are sleeping.
Knowing that it's far too late to force their heads
above,
but praying that we'll overcome the Sickness
with our Love.

The ability to SEE is one that's truly earned, not
given.

A burden bore with caution by the dead among
us, living.
So often sought with vigour yet discarded when
it's found;
Truth, like fire, can warm a home or burn it
down.

When our hearts are broken and our homes are
divided,
we begin to realize by NOT deciding - we
decided.
They tell us that our ignorance will somehow
bring us bliss.
We close our eyes, we die inside. Filing onboard
the sinking ship.

Yet, some of us are standing tall and singing
through the flames.
Some of us are learning how to float in crashing
waves.
Because we can't have ignorance without
choosing to ignore;
it's choosing not to contemplate - or, to reject
what's not yet known.

The Sickness knows how's easy it can be to gain
consent
from programmed minds who chime in time;
whose thoughts and words are bent.

Our sails cast with winds of change; our heat
reflects the sun.
Our broken hearts are rich with boundless
CARE,
of which the Sickness can know none.

Belly of the Beast

The Sickness has a centerpoint from which it
spirals out.
Infecting minds with spiral lies, designed for
casting doubt.
Tired stories, play-by-play for children from
another age.
Phantom models (hardly living) wear their virtue
on display.

Twisting, winding, sickening - the Sickness
makes its way.
Degenerate; their audience will cash their
cheque another day.
Their virtue lines the coffin that will close over
our hearts,
yet still we rank and file to the players and their
parts.

Analyzing every scene as if it's something real;
Never seeing while we do so, THEY control the
way we feel.
These characters which multiply like mindless
forms will do,
will occupy the minds of our all children - and
of you.

Inverted ways will leave their scars on every
soul they touch,
as the Sickness works to vandalize the things we
love so much.
As we applaud the final bow, and some will beg
for "more",
we stop to thank the ones who brought Sickness
through our door.

Mischievous, disguised as us - pretending they
can care.
But peer inside, behind their eyes, and see that
they're not there.
Without their spells and magic screen, they
appear as truly weak.
Still to learn that words return with vengeance
when we speak.

Without their masks and costumes, their forms
are truly vile;
a poor substitute for virtue with their shallow,
lifeless smiles.

Closed Circuit Man

Men in rows like herded animals.
Separated - made ashamed of what is natural.
These men have been fractured, distorted,
converted.

Denial of Truth makes purpose inverted.
Manipulation of Will means desire perverted.

Unsure, indirect - strangled by intellect.
Powerless to self-direct.
Preferring not to recollect.
Castrated by indifference.

Their longing gaze rests a moment too long, yet
you can't meet their eyes when their mind has
gone wrong.
They hide inside and give away
what can't abide - what they choose not to say.

Four structured walls blocking man from his
role,
so he settles for liquor, white powder and
football.
In sandals and khakis, hunting store-aisle prey;

trading purpose for barbeque meat on a
weekday.

For a red-lipped smile or a sideways look - a
man will sell his soul.
For the promise of a dollar bill, a man will give
it all.

For the one who buys to hypnotize away his own
free will,
will find in time his allies' friendly fire shoots to
kill.
For the one who chooses not to FEEL, and
chooses not to SPEAK;
the Sickness will pursue him all day long, and in
his sleep.

And if he should avert his eyes each time his
hand does wrong,
its certain that the Sickness will consume him
before long.

No More Natural Woman

Slow down, woman - you're in danger.
This disappearing act reflecting chaos in the
mirror.
Perfectly unbalanced, with silence on reserve.
The "right" thing, the "wrong" thing; a method
or a word.

The Sickness is chasing the mother, the sister.
Modelling the unreal, the broken - the sinister.
Collective division that splits through her heart,
confusing her senses and worth from the start.

Comparative nonsense and noise drowns her
voice,
as she's gaining AND losing her freedom of
choice.
Her beauty is guilty of nothing it's earned,
and though she knows better - she always
returns.

Til faced with such an unnatural witness;

delusion disguised as emotional fitness.
Til the leaders have fallen and surrendered their
badge;
or her children are calling but she can't go back.

Til the fire is burning but her heart is too sad.
Til the years have transformed the grass into
sand.
Til the muscles won't move - til the smile is
fixed.
Yet nobody is fooled by the scowl on her lips.

For a chance to shut down like the actors in
progress;
a sick cycling machine, from which the sick
profit.
But if she's truly bold enough to somehow stand
apart;
her goodness and her courage may repair her
broken heart.

Deviant's Delight

Age one, two, three. Indoctrinate your family.
Age four, five, six. The Sickness on the TV
screen.
Age seven, eight, nine. Snapping photos for your
timeline.

Every time, it's ballistic.
Secrets out - now we know;
the thing that caused it cannot fix it.

Look again, you must have missed it.
There's really no such thing as "princess" and
the "princes" are sadistic.

They're complicating matters when their
innocence is shattered.

Because we failed to protect them.
Instead, we volunteered to let them.

Inside the previous homes we made;
our cut-glass beds upon we laid.
In our medicated haze, we fail to justify our
ways.

But not without the consequence
of generations left with no defence.
Because we sorely, sickly faltered;
left our children at the alter.

Those tiny hands, those glistening eyes.
Wave good-bye, now. Wave goodnight.

Those precious, helpless human lives.
Wave good-bye, now. Wave goodnight.

And still we laugh when we should cry.
Wave good-bye, now. Wave goodnight.

Hypnotic Rhythm

Not the beat or dance of a number.
Instead, droning on (and on) the instrument of
slumber.
A waking rhythmic stupor to pacify the masses;
Reinforced by all the models - and the programs,
and the classes.

Not worthy of their virtue, but witlessly efficient
at destroying our potential, and making us
deficient.
Repeating ad nauseum the lies til they stick,
never knowing how harmful they are when they
speak.

Re-coding our make up with spell-casting
phrases;
subdividing our aspects in categorical mazes.
Confusing our senses to the point they're a scar
on the faces of stone; we forgot who we are.

The Sickness is tricky, manifesting its forms.
Deceiving and twisting our cultural norms.
Inverting, collapsing, and shrinking our wealth;
diluting, trapping, and poisoning our health.

If perception if projection, then suggestion
makes both;
(bound by the chains of the words that they
spoke).
Overriding our senses with what's not truly
there,
resting our future on the few left who CARE.

To make right the balance and settle the poles,
the many who follow must go with the flow.
When the concrete is rubble and the gardens
have died,
they'll finally see what's been there all this time.

Denying the rhythm of the spirit of rejection.
We'll stitch up the wounds and clear the
infection.
Slowly rebuilding the new way back home,
making natural music wherever we go.

Invisible Building Material

Here's an invitation - It's essential.
Deprogramming is necessary to reach your
potential.
Memory banks security code lifted;
time to retrieve the strength you've been gifted.

Real eyes realize real lies - it's time to unwind
impressions playing on repeat, defiling your
mind.
Placed inside a cage they dictated,
with just enough choices to mask how deeply
you hate it.

Monogrammed uniform - no windows, no
colour.
Hide the way that they shamed you and made
you another.
Alters inside running time slow or faster;
mimicking forms of unnatural masters.

Invisible programs play invisible games.

"Too little, too late". It's on a cycle again.
Many are lost; many willingly taken.
Many will sleep til the earthquakes come wake
them.

Unnatural forms need unnatural maintenance;
a type of hypnosis they use to seem ageless.
But there is a space where the Sickness can't
hide
from the aspect of Truth which will always
reside.

And there in that space lies the true moral key,
for the ones who can FEEL and desire to SEE.
We must be discerning of righteous defiance
towards makers of chaos and promoters of
violence.

Walls are not needed to build every cage
when the architect's watching from somewhere
backstage.
But when the picture is colour (and not black
and white),
the true form of the Sickness will fear for its life.

Its pillars will fall with the weight of the Truth;
for in time, every lie must be weighed against
proof.

And when the people SEE the lies,
the Sickness either grows or dies.

That hateful seed from ancient times
will loose its hold on all their minds.
And those who've occupied their eyes
will find their altars cracked and dry.

Actor-Based Reality

"Why does it matter?", they ask. "Why should I
care?"
With mild irritation or a dull, lifeless stare.
"This isn't a conversation that we want to have."
Can't see it. Won't hear it - assume you've gone
mad.

"Where'd you hear that? That's not true, I don't
believe it.
Who could be so evil? I don't know. I can't
conceive it."

They're sipping their coffee and telling their
stories
while the Sickness advances, progressively
forward.
Stalking their windows, leaking through all their
screens;
making them restless and stealing their sleep.

Making them fearful and breaking their will
til they go to their doctor and ask for some pills.

Multiple masks playing multiple roles.

Multiple stories with multiple holes.
Multiple ribbons and shining awards.
Lifeless disguises - deceiving for sport.

The actors dictating the roles we will play;
layering spells in the words that they say.
Still we offer our children and ourselves to their
alter;
not believing our heroes and idols can falter.

Too busy to raise them, we give up our time
to the Sickness. (We pay them) to live in our
mind.
Distorting our values and making us weak;
shallow, perverted, entitled and bleak.

Movies in movies and dreams inside dreams.
Confusing til nothing is quite as it seems.
Copying models we thought had the answer
but finding too often a void at the center.

It's hard to imagine, and harder to see
the system the Sickness was created to be.
Discernment is needed for both Freedom and
Peace;
and we'll discern neither til we get off our knees.

Symbols and Anchors

Language is a secret code for those among us "in
the know".
Binding blessings as they go; loosing chaos from
below.
Would you believe how deep it goes?
Are your eyes open, blank or closed?

Or filled with fear as such they find
for those who dedicate their mind
to watching programs all the time;
whose heads are filled with death and crime.

Until the final curtain falls
like torrents from a waterfall;
their eyes will twist the screens they see,
their ears will trick them easily.

They've given up the proper use
of senses that we can't confuse
with programs and impulsive thoughts;
with leaders that we should have fought.

Because their voice begins to rot
as words collapse the forms they bought.
Because they can't escape their own;
like poison ivy - overgrown.

Still the Sickness wears its toll - still dominates
the Superbowl.
Still weighs a heavy veil of grief
to "entertain" or make us sleep.

When the ritual ends and the spells have been
made,
each one will arise from the bed where we've
laid.
And though many voices will defend their
position,
the Truth will expose who is truly convicted.

Whose hand is still hidden?
Whose gold are they after?
Black and white puppets
serving black and white masters.

Not choosing IS choosing.
Soon many will know
every action is counted
when our harvest is sown.

Identity Thieves

Psychological operations;
modern history, trauma-based nation.
High strangeness, all-seeing eye
dividing lines for multidimensional eyes.

Riding high on blood trails and chemicals.
Generations of programmed, hack-able animals.
Inverting the stories til they no longer make
sense
and burying the buildings along with the Reset.

Creating a script that is controlling and foul;
deploying the people against their own power.
Attacking the human biological roots
in order to make something new they can use.

Some call it transhuman; some call it eugenics.
Some call it science and some outright reject it.
But one thing's for certain, we'll see before long
if we've earned the right and privilege to play
God.

Designing a new thing whose senses are weak;
confusion distorting the words that they speak.
Inverting the body, inverting the mind;

we've seen this before - over and over in time.

When the balance is broken to the point it can't
right,
then Nature will enter and shine forth her light.
But nature is vicious (as soon we will know);
even the Sickness will burn in her glow.

And if you can make it - if you can climb out,
it's only the Sickness that you'll be without.
Because what you've left will have wasted away,
and the Truth will reward you with Freedom,
one day.

Sick Composition

The Sickness is both an entity and delusion.
A psychotic compulsion; a spell of confusion.
Parasitic in nature - it's constantly needing
to feed and to breed inside of human beings.

Mirroring, copying; imitating real faces
in order to access useful people and places.
By seizing the Will, and making complacent;
binding our minds with a cord that is ancient.

Same techniques on different screens.
Repeating every mis-recorded scene.
Repetition reigns supreme to advance in their
degree;
nothing hidden carries value which will truly
make them free.

Knowledge is common but wisdom is rare.
Belief and experience are both subject to Care.

Symbolic Language

Using symbols to communicate and mediate
what they instigate.
Subconsciously retrieve the state,
repeating til they break the gate.

And down the walls of senses fall
until they hardly work at all.
Pretend you never heard the call;
you can't discern - you've become dull.

Tricky actors wearing masks
with hands occupied by harmful acts.
Hidden things that few will know,
in hidden places few will go.

Pushing symbols up the tower.
Looking for that other power.
Parasites do power seek
to hide the need that makes them weak.

That endless, vacant starving need
to terrorize the human being.
Compassion void before the throne;
no magic spell can take them home.

However bound, they too can bind
the soul whose virtue left behind.
They seed the illness in your mind.
Illusions from behind your eyes.

Identities on which they feed
need greater hands to be released.
Beyond what magic can define;
to recognize what is divine.

They Must Be Drugged

"They will be sick - they must be drugged.
We have products; pills and treatments.
Commodities with human needs
in need of us to meet them."

In turn, the word for "cure" is banned so only
"sick" can foster.
If a doctor cures a man, they'll simply call him
an imposter.
No "cure" can ever take the place of a treatment
sold at profit;
because if healing was believed then everyone
would want it.

So, the Sickness and its hosts
infect the treatments coast to coast.
It vilifies what nature made;
the price of life and death is paid.

De-Programming Is Necessary

Our masks will be stripped away by their
passage;
unnatural forms and unnatural language.
The world is not fixed - hypnotic rhythm and
suggestion.
What you see here changes form when you use
your mind to question.

The eye opens naturally when the mind is fixed
on Truth;
so they try to bind the eye, beginning in our
youth.
Mind control and doublespeak - patterns on the
screen.
Suggestions made repeatedly until you want to
scream.

Inversion is preferred to use, in order to deceive,
Creating cognitive dissonance for the programs
to relieve.
Programmed speech, directed mind -
subconscious influence.

Rejecting lies and programmed ties becomes our
first line of defence.

Fragmentation realized; altered states to go
unnoticed;
except by those who use their eyes and see the
truth before us.
Deception may already be the preferred method
of control;
but to accept the Sickness by default will cost
each one of us our soul.

De-programming increases flexibility in the
inner system.
Acute toxicity is the agent of imprisonment to
our senses.
Truth is the method used to reverse inversion;
and virtue is the value which will upset this
whole diversion.

Local Control Grid

Locality, identity.
Manipulate the senses.
Relieve responsibility.
Replace sovereignty with entertainment.

It's normal to feel uneasy
in an environment that's breaking.
But the Sickness tells you that you're broken
or worse - that you're just faking.

Identity, malady.
Conforming to the Sickness.
Turn off the news to realize
the stand you made to witness.

Locality matters - this isn't a drill.
But the Sickness confuses our heart and our will.
Hypnotic suggestion - the program is laid.
Deciding decisions we haven't yet made.

Masquerading as monarchs (elevated elites);
never feeling the cool earth supporting their feet.
Never seeing the Truth that will turn them
around.

Never satisfied to rest in the position they're
found.

Always squirming and leering, designing their
play;
because the Sickness decides every part of their
day.
A pitiful role for a second-rate actor;
played beyond what is human for a second-rate
master.

The Antidote

The end of rapture and its deceptive allure.
Living in painting and movies we forgot to
watch.
Living in oceans of feelings like crashing waves.
We touch every coastline; we speak with every
tree and stone.

Ever reaching, arms wide.
Heart open, eyes open.
Palms outstretched.
Our creation is pure and our gratitude deep.

We live in joy of our making, strengthened by
faith;
and empowered in our conviction
that the time we are given is infinitely precious.

Reality Standard Time

There is nothing outside Now.
So Then could not have been
if not Now in this moment
of seamless union with the Future.

This being the rare and beautiful gift of the
Present.

www.ingramcontent.com/pod-product-compliance
Lightning Source LLC
La Vergne TN
LVHW010924200726
843509LV00013B/2052